R•M ROYAL ONTARIO MUSEUM

THE FORBIDDEN CITY

INSIDE THE COURT OF CHINA'S EMPERORS

WEN-CHIEN CHENG   CHEN SHEN

WITH CONTRIBUTIONS FROM SARAH FEE

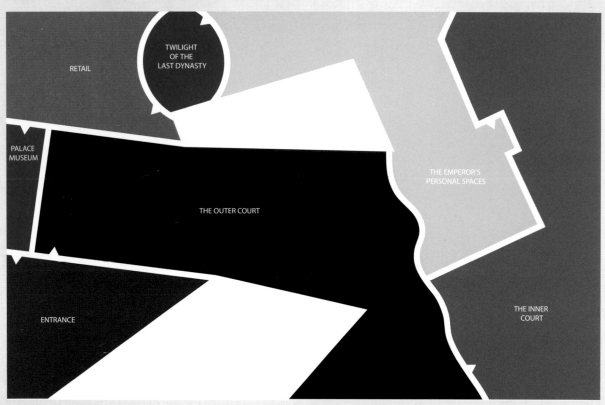

RETAIL

TWILIGHT
OF THE
LAST DYNASTY

PALACE
MUSEUM

THE EMPEROR'S
PERSONAL SPACES

THE OUTER COURT

THE INNER
COURT

ENTRANCE

exhibition floor plan

CONTENTS

24 EMPERORS LIVED AND RULED FROM THE FORBIDDEN CITY

MING DYNASTY (1368–1644)

REIGN NAME	PERSONAL NAME	TEMPLE NAME	REIGN YEARS
Emperor Yongle (永樂)	Zhu Di (朱棣)	Chengzu (成祖)	1403–1424
Emperor Hongxi (洪熙)	Zhu Gaochi (朱高熾)	Renzong (仁宗)	1425
Emperor Xuande (宣德)	Zhu Zhanji (朱瞻基)	Xuanzong (宣宗)	1426–1435
Emperor Zhengtong (正統)	Zhu Qizhen (朱祁鎮)	Yingzong (英宗)	1436–1449
Emperor Jingtai (景泰)	Zhu Qiyu (朱祁鈺)	Daizong (代宗)	1450–1456
Emperor Tianshun (天順)	Zhu Qizhen (朱祁鎮)	Yingzong (英宗)	1457–1464
Emperor Chenghua (成化)	Zhu Jianshen (朱見深)	Xianzong (憲宗)	1465–1487
Emperor Hongzhi (弘治)	Zhu Youtang (朱祐樘)	Xiaozong (孝宗)	1488–1505
Emperor Zhengde (正德)	Zhu Houzhao (朱厚照)	Wuzong (武宗)	1506–1521
Emperor Jiajing (嘉靖)	Zhu Houcong (朱厚熜)	Shizong (世宗)	1522–1566
Emperor Longqing (隆慶)	Zhu Zaihou (朱載垕)	Muzong (穆宗)	1567–1572
Emperor Wanli (萬曆)	Zhu Yijun (朱翊鈞)	Shenzong (神宗)	1573–1620
Emperor Taichang (泰昌)	Zhu Changluo (朱常洛)	Guangzong (光宗)	1620
Emperor Tianqi (天啟)	Zhu Youjiao (朱由校)	Xizong (熹宗)	1621–1627
Emperor Chongzhen (崇禎)	Zhu Youjian (朱由檢)	Sizong (思宗)	1628–1644

QING DYNASTY
(1644–1912)

REIGN NAME	PERSONAL NAME	TEMPLE NAME	REIGN YEARS
Emperor Shunzhi (順治)	Fulin (福臨)	Shizu (世祖)	1644–1661
Emperor Kangxi (康熙)	Xuanye (玄燁)	Shengzu (聖祖)	1662–1722
Emperor Yongzheng (雍正)	Yinzhen (胤禛)	Shizong (世宗)	1723–1735
Emperor Qianlong (乾隆)	Hongli (弘曆)	Gaozong (高宗)	1736–1795
Emperor Jiaqing (嘉慶)	Yongyan (顒琰)	Renzong (仁宗)	1796–1820
Emperor Daoguang (道光)	Minning (旻寧)	Xuanzong (宣宗)	1821–1850
Emperor Xianfeng (咸豐)	Yizhu (奕詝)	Wenzong (文宗)	1851–1861
Emperor Tongzhi (同治)	Zaichun (載淳)	Muzong (穆宗)	1862–1874
Emperor Guangxu (光绪)	Zaitian (載湉)	Dezong (德宗)	1875–1908
Emperor Xuantong (宣統)	Puyi (溥儀)	none given	1909–1912

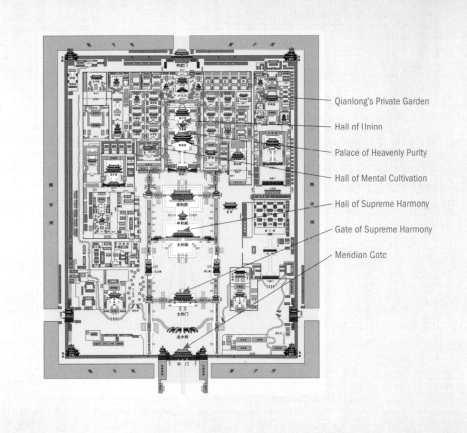

Qianlong's Private Garden

Hall of Union

Palace of Heavenly Purity

Hall of Mental Cultivation

Hall of Supreme Harmony

Gate of Supreme Harmony

Meridian Gate

FOREWORD

As the twenty-first century ushers in an integrated global culture, the Royal Ontario Museum continues to connect visitors to their world and each other. This year marks the hundredth anniversary of the ROM's existence and we are proud to feature *The Forbidden City: Inside the Court of China's Emperors* as our special Centennial exhibition. In collaboration with Beijing's Palace Museum, the ROM brings to Canada the relics of a momentous chapter in China's long and fascinating history. For the first time, Canadians will encounter treasures that were part of Chinese imperial life for six centuries in a city strictly off-limits to all but the emperor, his family, and thousands of his servants.

Our exhibition takes visitors on a remarkable journey to the heart of the Forbidden City, eventually to the personal study of the Emperor where few have ever been. With incredibly rare artifacts from Beijing's Palace Museum, augmented by objects from the ROM's own renowned collections, we tell the extraordinary stories and reveal the characters that, for centuries, made the Forbidden City the compelling centre of an immense empire.

We are especially grateful to The Robert H. N. Ho Family Foundation as the Presenting Sponsor and Manulife as the Lead Sponsor for their generous support of this exhibition. Special thanks also to the Palace Museum, for collaborating with our curators and allowing us display these priceless royal artifacts, some of which have never left the Palace before. As always, we are indebted to the Louise Hawley Stone Charitable Trust for their continued support of our publications, which enables us to produce this exhibition guide.

I would like to thank the exhibition's lead curator Dr. Chen Shen along with co-curator Dr. Wen-chien Cheng and advisory curator Dr. Sarah Fee for the hard work and long hours that they put into the making of this exquisite exhibition. For centuries the Forbidden City has fascinated the world, and we are extremely pleased to begin our Centennial celebrations by bringing to our visitors Chinese national treasures from this cultural and historic landmark.

Janet Carding
President and CEO, Royal Ontario Museum

INTRODUCTION

THE FORBIDDEN CITY:
HOME OF CHINA'S LAST EMPERORS

The place where earth and sky meet, where the four seasons merge, where wind and rain are gathered in, and where Yang *and* Yin *are in harmony.*[1]

In ancient Chinese thought, the emperor was the central figure in his empire, a place known as the "middle kingdom" and located at the very centre of the universe. The emperor's residence was built at the heart of the imperial capital as a symbol of this centrality. The location of his residence also corresponded to the position of the North Star or Ziwei yuan 紫微垣 (Purple Numinous Star), which in the ancient Chinese constellations is the home of the celestial god Taiyi 太乙. Ancient Chinese believed that the ever-constant Ziwei yuan was aligned with the central axis of the universe and all other stars revolved around it. This celestial connection gave birth to the idea that the emperor's residence was a Heavenly Palace on Earth. Chinese emperors sustained the harmony between nature and heaven and so were considered heaven's sons. Over the last

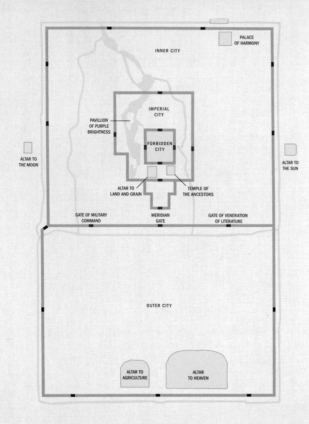

INNER CITY

PALACE OF HARMONY

IMPERIAL CITY

PAVILLION OF PURPLE BRIGHTNESS

FORBIDDEN CITY

ALTAR TO THE MOON

ALTAR TO THE SUN

ALTAR TO LAND AND GRAIN

TEMPLE OF THE ANCESTORS

GATE OF MILITARY COMMAND

MERIDIAN GATE

GATE OF VENERATION OF LITERATURE

OUTER CITY

ALTAR TO AGRICULTURE

ALTAR TO HEAVEN

two dynasties, Ming 明 and Qing 清, Chinese people called the imperial palace Zijin cheng 紫禁城. When translated into English it became known as the Forbidden City. The palace's Chinese name was conceived to associate it with a heavenly place (the Purple Numinous Star; *zi* means "noble colour purple")—a dwelling on earth that was heavily guarded or restricted (*jin*) and designed like a walled city (*cheng*).

The Forbidden City is located in Beijing 北京, which did not become a capital city until the thirteenth century, when the Mongol empire first established its royal palace there. During the Ming and Qing dynasties, Beijing was a city of walls within walls, one of several design concepts preserved from ancient Chinese capital cities. The structure of the city included four enclosures. From its core outwards it was divided into the Palace City or Forbidden City (for the imperial court and residence), the Imperial City (for royal administrative functions and other amenities),

Fig. 1. Major districts in the Qing dynasty Beijing, showing the position of the Forbidden City. Illustration based on map from *China: The Three Emperors 1662-1795*.

the Inner City (for the residences of noble families and offices of state administrators), and the Outer City (for commoners' residences and markets) (fig. 1). All were regulated by rigid restrictions. The centralized axis line and symmetric layout of all the buildings in the Forbidden City are an important part of its spirit. From the Hall of Supreme Harmony (Taihe dian 太和殿) in the centre of the city, the axis line runs north and south and extends outside and along Beijing's primary gateway. An unusual Qing dynasty bird's-eye view painting of the capital in spring, as seen in the exhibition, provides an artistic contemporary view of this vibrant city (fig. 2).

The Forbidden City was first built according to the vision of Zhu Di 朱棣, the third emperor of the Ming dynasty whose original base of power was in Beijing. Before Zhu Di ascended to the throne (ca. 1403) the Ming capital was located in the south, in Nanjing 南京. Three years after becoming emperor Zhu Di relocated his primary residence and administrative centre to the north,

Fig. 2. Xu Yang, Bird's-eye view of the capital city, inspired by Emperor Qianlong's poems

where he began his ambitious plan to build the Forbidden City. Construction lasted for 14 years and involved over one million labourers. Completed in 1420, the Forbidden City served as the residence to royal families and the headquarters of China's last two dynasties. Its primarily wooden architecture made it difficult to maintain. Over the many years of their existence, the buildings went through expansions, fires, reconstructions, and renovations. The present-day layout largely matches what the city might have looked like during the reign of Emperor Qianlong 乾隆 (r. 1736–1795).

The central location and calculated architectural design of the palaces served to highlight the authority of the mandated rulers and marked this as their rightful place to rule. Considered the world's largest palace complex, the Forbidden City has an amazing floor plan: nearly 90 palace complexes, 980 buildings, and about 9,000 rooms, all occupying 720,000 square metres. The buildings were no doubt the tallest and largest in the capital. Their shining roof tiles were yellow—a colour used exclusively by the royal family because it symbolized the supreme

power of the imperial reign. The splendour of the palace halls, when they were completed in the early fifteenth century, must have dazzled the officials and court audiences attending the opening ceremonies. One Ming official present described the following:

Jade-white tablets glitter in the sun; jewelled columns soar towards the sky. The golden pavement glistens; the lattice windows are delicately carved. Pearls and jade radiate with their lustre . . . [2]

The Forbidden City was divided into a public or Outer Court (*waichao* 外朝) in the south and the private quarters of the emperor and his family, an Inner Court (*neiting* 內庭), in the north. In the Outer Court there are three grand, formal throne halls along with open courtyards. Here emperors would receive homage from only selected subjects and foreign envoys. This is also where state ceremonies and inaugurations took place. During Emperor Qianlong's reign, a magnificently large painting depicted one such monumental event, which took place in front of the Gate of Supreme Harmony (Taihe men 太和門)—hundreds of envoys brought New Year's gifts to the Emperor (fig. 3). The Inner Court was reserved for only a handful of selected high offices. Princes (who had to move out of the Forbidden City once they were married adults) entered only for daily official business. The Inner Court also served as the residence of the emperor and his immediate family, as well as the servants, eunuchs, and maids who attended to the daily needs of the imperial family.

The residents of the Forbidden City included both the Han and their non-Han rulers, the Manchu. The Han were the Chinese who established the Ming dynasty by conquering the nomadic rulers of the Yuan dynasty. The Manchu originated in northeast Asia and overthrew the Ming to found the last alien-conquest regime in imperial China. While never shedding their Manchu identity and purposely maintaining their distinctive Eight-Banners

Fig. 3. Anonymous court painters, *Envoys from Subordinate States and Foreign Countries Presenting Tribute to the Emperor*

military–social system, the Manchu rulers adopted the Han culture and Confucian canon as the foundation of their political rule. They patronized Chinese art and literature, winning over the Han literati-elite and safeguarding precious treasures from previous imperial collections. As emperors of the last dynasty, they inherited incomparable material culture of the court that had been passed down for centuries. The objects remaining in the Forbidden City reflected more than just the tastes of emperors who resided there, but the most refined artistic standards throughout ages, the succeeding aesthetics of court life, and the continuity and changing trends in society.

ABOUT THE EXHIBITION

Built more than 600 hundred years ago, the Forbidden City remained a mysterious and privileged locale, accessible only to imperial families and selected officials, guests, and servants before the republican era. Today, the largest palace in the world is one of the most visited world heritage destinations. For the first time in Canada, the exhibition *The Forbidden City: Inside the Court of China's Emperors* brings the Forbidden City to life by showcasing approximately 250 of the finest, most appealing and narratively rich objects, all on loan from the Palace Museum, Beijing. In addition to being enormous in scale, this exceptional exhibition includes more than 80 artifacts that have never travelled outside the Forbidden City.

The exhibition was developed by ROM curators, in consultation with the Palace Museum, to provide a detailed look at life inside the imperial palace. Although the exhibition focuses heavily on the Qing period, with the majority of objects on view originally belonging to the Qing court (due to limits on the availability of objects on loan from the Palace Museum), it does represent imperial court culture as a whole, which was a dominant feature of the Qing as well as former Chinese dynasties. Objects have been specially selected for their artistic significance and for the purpose of illuminating the storylines woven through the exhibition. The result is an impressive display of artifacts, ranging from exquisite and opulent treasures, artworks, and instruments, to rare or one-of-a-kind daily objects. All of the works-on-paper and textiles will be rotated at the mid-point of the exhibition's six-month display period, due to conservation requirements.

The layout of the exhibition marginally follows the architectural design of the actual palace space and echoes the structural concept of the Forbidden City. We begin with an outsider's view. General historical information and the symbolism of the Forbidden City are presented in "Outside the Forbidden City," which invites visitors to further explore the once-forbidden space. Upon entering the largest component of the exhibition, "Inside the Forbidden City," one progresses through three continuous sections: the Outer Court, the Inner Court, and the Emperor's Personal Spaces. Life inside the court corresponded with the conceptual design of the city: the outer was more public and ceremonial, the inner was more private, informal, and exclusive. The section corresponding to the Outer Court is meant to impress the viewer with its imperial grandeur, power, privilege, and ritual solemnity. Here one experiences through objects grand public events, such as state ceremonials (pages 32, 34, 36), imperial weddings (pages 30–31, 59), birthdays (pages 23–26, 28–29), New Year celebrations, and royal hunting. Moving into the private space of the everyday lives of emperors and their families, the viewer experiences a sense of voyeurism through a more intimate display. One glimpses the informal aspects of imperial life, such as fashion (page 53–58), entertainment, mealtimes, and objects for daily use (page 59–61). Before leaving the Inner Court we are channelled into a unique section, "The emperor's Personal Spaces," where the Emperor's artistic cultivation and mind-blowing imperial treasures are dramatically showcased for our viewing enjoyment (pages 64–69). An additional area presents the Qing emperors' encounters with the western world. The concluding area, "The Twilight of the Last Dynasty," reveals the stories of the imperial palace's transformation into the Palace Museum as it is today, at the fall of the last empire and the beginning of the republican era.

Fig. 4. Packed artifacts await shipment in front of the Gate of Supreme Harmony during the Sino-Japanese War

treasures inside the Forbidden City were removed and transported to various locations for protection (fig. 4). The most dramatic move was to Taiwan, just before the fall of the Nationalist Party government and the communist takeover of China in 1949. Today, the treasures of the Forbidden City are divided among three locations—Taipei, Nanjing, and Beijing—but the Palace Museum still houses a collection of over 1.8 million objects. The Palace Museum continues its tireless efforts to locate and retrieve objects that once belonged to the City and to bring many of these treasures back to China (page 29). Without the Palace Museum's commitment to preserving these national treasures and making them available for public viewing, this exhibition would not be possible.

Wen-chien Cheng
Louise Hawley Stone Chair of Far Eastern Art

In 1925, after the revolution that ended the imperial era in China, the Forbidden City was turned into the Palace Museum, a public institute that opened the palace doors to all people. Because of the warfare and chaotic political circumstances of the early twentieth century in China, the

1   *Zhou Li*, chap. 3, quoted from Paul Wheatley, *The Pivot of the Four Quarters* (Edinburgh University Press, 1971), 428.
2   "Grand Ode on the Greatness of the Imperial Capital," by Yang Rong 楊榮 (1371–1440). Translated in English by Klaas Ruitenbeek.

EXHIBITION HIGHLIGHTS

POWER AND PRIVILEGE

Bowl
萬曆款黃釉碗

Porcelain with yellow glaze
Ming dynasty, Wanli mark and period
Royal Ontario Museum 2013.43.1

In almost every medium and form, the colour yellow was exclusively used for the imperial family. Utensils like this bowl were for everyday use in the Forbidden City, but bowls in imperial yellow (*minghuang* 明黄) were restricted to the emperor, empress dowager, and empress. Imperial consorts used yellow bowls with white interiors, while the high-rank concubines used yellow bowls with green dragons.

This rare yellow-glazed monochrome bowl was designed and commissioned by the court of Emperor Wanli, and made exclusively at the imperial kilns at Jingdezhen 景德鎮. Wanli, the thirteenth emperor of the Ming dynasty, ruled the country for over 40 years (1573–1620). During his reign, Manchu people living north of the Great Wall established the Qing dynasty, which became a political and military rival of the Ming court. The Qing took over the Ming court at the Forbidden City in 1644.

Plate with dragon design
嘉靖款黃地青花勾蓮大盤

Blue-and-white porcelain with overglazed yellow enamel.
Ming dynasty, Jiajing mark and period
The Palace Museum, Gu144700

Dragons were the ultimate symbol of imperial power and adorned many of the emperor's possessions, from everyday utensils to artwork and costumes, and even the palace itself. More than 12,600 dragon designs are said to have been incorporated into the architecture of the Forbidden City. The emperor's dragons were special, with features that identified them as imperial. One such feature is illustrated on this beautiful dish—only the emperor's dragons had five claws.

This is one of the finest early-Ming porcelains from the imperial kilns at Jingdezhen. Beyond its unusually large size, this plate was the rare product of a twice-glazed technique. First, the makers fired a common blue-and-white dish featuring a forward-facing dragon surrounded by intertwined lotus flowers. Then they covered the original white glaze with an iron-rich glaze and fired the dish again, this time at a lower temperature. The result was an imperial yellow background.

Ruyi charm
白玉紫檀如意

Jade and sandalwood
Qing dynasty, 18th–19th century
Royal Ontario Museum, 987.46.1

The *ruyi* 如意 was originally a Buddist monk's tool for back scratching, but subsequently evolved into a general lucky charm. In the Qing dynasty, the *ruyi* was the most common and important gift given to wish good fortune. The first gift that Emperor Qianlong gave to King George III via Lord George Macartney in 1793 was a jade *ruyi* charm.

During court celebrations, nobles and high-ranking officials presented the emperor and empress with *ruyi* charms as tokens of good wishes. This charm is made of three white jade panels decorated with fish and lotus motifs, and a sandalwood (*zitan* 紫檀) handle carved with five immortal elders standing among evergreen trees, a symbol of longevity. This *ruyi* was a birthday gift to Emperor Jiaqing, presented by Dong Gao 董誥 (1740–1818), a high-ranking official. Dong is well-known for his painting and calligraphy even in art markets today.

Set of the original 120 seals with their gift box

A pair of seal imprint albums
緙絲元音壽牒、寶典福書冊
Silk tapestry
Qing dynasty, Qianlong period
The Palace Museum, Gu72834, Gu72829

The year 1790 marked an important event in the Qing dynasty: the 80th birthday of Emperor Qianlong, the only Chinese emperor to live beyond this age. The Chief Grand Councillor, He Shen 和珅 (1750–1799), who was also the emperor's favourite official, selected 120 auspicious phrases from Emperor Qianlong's own poems and essays. These phrases were then carved into 120 seals, each with a different design, and presented to the emperor as a gift.

Hu Jitang 胡季堂 (1729–1800), then the Minister of Justice (*xibu shangshu* 刑部尚書), commissioned his own personal gift to Qianlong: two albums made of cut-silk tapestry (*kesi* 緙絲), which is a very special and unique silk weaving technique in ancient China. Each album has sixteen fold-out pages into which are woven the imprints in the exact style of the original seals with a transcription above each seal. Each phrase consists of three to eight characters; in one album, each phrase contains the character for "longevity" (*shou* 壽), whereas each phrase in the other album include the character for "luck" (*fu* 福).

Hu Jitang became one of the top court officials during the reign of Emperor Jiaqing, and helped the emperor to take down He Shen, the most corrupt official of Emperor Qianlong's time. Hu confiscated 40 tons of grains from He Shen's estate and redistributed it to the starving survivors of natural disasters in two counties.

near right: The title pages of the albums

far right, top: The inscription on the last page reads: "Hu Jitang, the Minister, respectfully presents this to the Emperor on the First Day of Qianlong year *gengxu*, in celebration of His Majesty's 80th birthday."

far right, bottom: One of the fold-out pages shows eight phrases, each containing the same *fu* character.

Cup and saucer

金盞花嵌珍珠杯盤

Gold and pearls
Qing dynasty
The Palace Museum, Gu12130

The emperor drank from this gold cup and saucer at his birthday celebration. As he did, he saw the symbols of birthday wishes reserved only for an emperor or empress.

Characters were carved into the open-work handles: *wanshou* 萬壽, meaning "ten thousand years of longevity," and *wujiang* 無疆, or "eternal long life," a message reinforced by the ganoderma mushroom carved below the characters. Five-clawed dragons adorn the cup and saucer, surrounded by clouds and lotus flowers. Pearls add to the cup's exquisite beauty.

Imperial throne set

紅雕漆嵌玉荷花紋寶座

Lacquer, jade, ivory, silk, feathers, and cloisonné enamel
Qing dynasty, Qianlong period
The Palace Museum, Gu115711

When the emperor met with officials and guests at various formal events, it was important that he appear above them—literally—to convey his heavenly status. The Forbidden City's formal throne halls and the residential hall of each emperor or empress contained an elaborate imperial throne setting. Since the Outer Court was where the emperor presented his power to the world, the thrones in the Inner Court were less lavish but more lovely, like this one.

Being comfortable was less important to the emperor than portraying power, so the red-lacquered seat of the throne and the three-panelled screen behind it were made wider and deeper than they needed to be. The full setting included fans on elephant stands, crane candleholders, and sensors in the shape of lions, *luduan* 甪端 (a mythical animal), and pagodas—a grouping forbidden to anyone but the emperor, empress dowager, and empress.

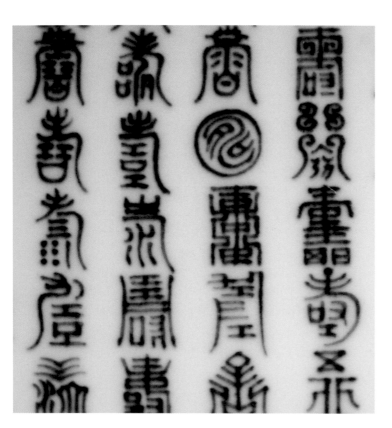

Vase with ten thousand *shou* characters and brush pen holder

青花萬壽字尊, 青花題 "萬壽尊賦" 筆筒

Porcelain with blue underglaze
Qing dynasty, Kangxi mark and period
The Palace Museum, Gu156997, Xin204849

Emperor Kangxi, who ascended to the throne at the age of 8, received this vase as a gift on his 60th birthday, in 1714. The blue-and-white vase is decorated with a single character—*shou* 壽 (longevity)—repeated 10,000 times in 975 different styles. The number 10,000 (*wan* 萬) was itself a blessing: it was the highest unit in Chinese accounting, signifying eternal life.

The brush pen holder displayed nearby was made in the imperial kiln at Jingdezhen, and is uniquely decorated with a long essay entitled "Wanshouzun fu" 萬壽尊賦 ("verse for *zun* vase of ten thousand *shou*"). The ware was particularly made to praise the vase above. For reasons unknown, likely as an imperial gift to the guests, the pen holder was taken from the palace. The Palace Museum acquired this antiquity in 2012, thus reuniting it with the vase after nearly 300 years.

Two Plates and One Bowl

吉祥如意款粉彩歲朝嬰戲圖大盤

喜字大盤, 喜字碗

Porcelain
Qing dynasty, Tongzhi mark and period
The Palace Museum, Gu156234,
Royal Ontario Museum 995.146.7-8

Emperor Tongzhi was one of only four Qing emperors who were married in the Forbidden City while on the throne. For his wedding, the Imperial Household Department (*neiwufu* 內務府) commissioned 10,072 wedding wares to be made in the imperial kilns at Jingdezhen over the course of five years leading up to the wedding in 1872. Of the surviving wares, 3,019 are in today's Palace Museum collection. Others are in collections outside China, including these two (left) at the Royal Ontario Museum.

The large pictorial plate (right) is one of two such plates in the Palace Museum's collection of wedding ware that feature children playing.

It displays auspicious characters suitable for a wedding, such as "double happiness" (also seen on the ROM's plate) and "good fortune and felicity." The scene pictured is of 100 children enjoying various games and entertainments. Some are playing "running land boat," "dragon dance," and "animal lantern," and others are playing with firecrackers.

Taicu bell

Taicu chime

Taicu bronze bell and *Taicu* jade chime stone
銅鍍金鑄鐘-太簇, 碧玉描金特磬-太簇
Bronze and jade with wood stand
Qing dynasty, Qianlong period, 1761
The Palace Museum, Gu169493, Gu169300 3/12

Taicu 太簇 is the name for one of 12 musical tones. In 1761, Emperor Qianlong ordered a set of 12 bells made, one for each tone. The bells were based on an ancient form, the *bo* 鎛 bell, that had been unearthed two years earlier. In that same year, the emperor had a set of jade chimes made, each from a single nodule of nephrite jade transported from the mountains in Hetian 和闐. Each chime was to be paired with a bell, and both would be played with other full sets (16 tones) of bells and chimes. The court orchestra used a different pair of bronze bell and jade chime for each month of the lunar year; *Taicu* bell and chime were used in the first month. When the orchestra played, the musical "conversation" began with a single strike of a *bo* bell; and ended with just one chime.

Two *Dacheng* bells

大晟鐘-黃鐘; 大晟鐘- 無射

Bronze
Song dynasty, Huizong period, 1100–1126
The Palace Museum, Gu77858; Royal Ontario Museum, 933.12.212

In 1104, Emperor Huizong 徽宗 of the Song dynasty ordered 336 bells to be made, in the exact form of ancient bells that prevailed during the East Zhou (771–256 BCE). The name *Dacheng* 大晟 was inscribed on the front of each bell, while the name of its tone appeared on the back panel. The ROM bell (far right) was among those brought to the Jin 金 dynasty (1115–1234) in northeast China along with captured Emperor Huizong after the fall of the Northern Song dynasty. Because the character *cheng* 晟 coincides with the name of the second emperor of the Jin dynasty, the court ordered the original name on the bell scratched off and a new name inscribed: *Dahe* 大和 (Great Harmony).

These bells became precious collectables for later dynasties. Today, only about 30 *Dacheng* bells survive, including these two—reunited for the first time in this exhibition.

Dacheng bell

Dacheng bell renamed "Dahe"

Ceremonial robe (autumn)
彩雲金龍紋男夾朝袍

Silk tapestry
Qing dynasty, Jiaqing period
The Palace Museum, Gu42489

Intricate codes of dress mandated by law applied to everyone from the emperor to the lowliest bureaucrat. The shape of a robe, as well as its colour, fibre of the fabric, symbols, and associated headgear, varied according to rank, gender, season, and event. Official, semi-official, and informal occasions each required different outfits.

For religious rites the emperor donned the most conservative dress: the ceremonial robe known as *chaofu* 朝服, characterized by a long-sleeved bodice affixed to a pleated skirt. Each of the four annual sacrifices called for a different colour and weight of fabric. The pale blue ("moon white") *chaofu* robe here would have been worn by the emperor for the sacrifice of the autumn equinox held at the Altar to the Moon (Yuetan 月壇), west of the Forbidden City. A silk label on the garment reveals it belonged to Emperor Jiaqing and was made with the highly esteemed *kesi* tapestry technique, which produces a fabric said to be worth its weight in gold.

Twelve-symbol semi-official robe
十二章吉服

Silk, gold thread
Qing dynasty, Qianlong period
Royal Ontario Museum, 909.12.2

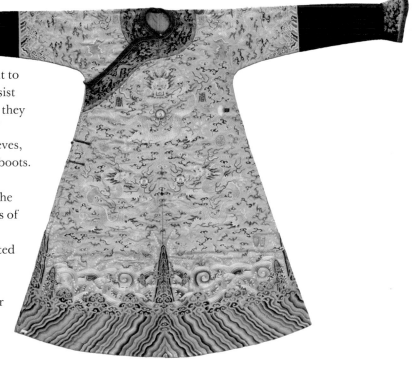

Dress was a major means by which Qing rulers sought to distinguish themselves from the Han majority and resist assimilation. Through various published dress codes, they imposed on the court a style of dress based on that of Manchu horsemen: narrow robes with slits, tight sleeves, "horse hoof" cuffs, and flared collars worn with riding boots.

Yet Qing emperors also appropriated elements of China's symbolic past, using dragons to distinguish the dress of the royal family. The Twelve Ancient Symbols of Imperial Authority embellished the emperor's robes. Dating to ancient Han times, these symbols represented the leader's virtues and powers, such as courage and wisdom. This semi-official twelve-symbol robe is rare because it has two signs—one was more common—for the constellations, which stood for the Emperor's ability to shed light. It was likely worn by the Emperor Qianlong.

Ceremonial armour and helmet

雍正帝御用棉甲，鐵金累絲盔

Cotton padding, silk satin, copper studs, metal plate, lacquered leather
Qing dynasty, Yongzheng period
The Palace Museum, Gu171802, Gu172262

The emperor's role as head of the military required special costume: a ceremonial suit of "armour." Worn for military reviews and troop inspections, and to awe potential enemies, it was made more for show than active battle.

This pale blue and golden set of armour was custom-made for Emperor Yongzheng. It is made in the multi-piece style that emerged in the late 18th century, with separate skirt, bodice, padded shoulders, sleeves, cuffs, collar, front flaps, and back flaps. Its ornamentation features large embroidered undulating golden dragons, clouds, water, and fire pearls; gold rivets; and a blue silk lining.

The imposing helmet is made of black lacquered leather. It is adorned with gold, coloured beads, and magical formulae written in Sanskrit and believed to have protective properties. Further extending the height of the helmet, but not shown here, is a finial comprised of a "plume" of black sable fur topped by pearls and carved gold beads.

Dexing sabre and scabbard
"德興" 款玉嵌寶石把金桃皮鞘腰刀

Steel blade with silver and gold, wood scabbard and fish skin
Qing dynasty, Qianlong period
The Palace Museum, Gu170401

To reflect the military skill of his Manchu heritage, Emperor Qianlong commissioned and maintained a collection of weaponry. This sabre, too ornate to be used in battle, was part of that collection. Qianlong himself designed and approved each piece; he classified them into three series: heaven (*tian* 天), earth (*di* 地), and people (*ren* 人). The emperor ordered a total of 60 ceremonial curved swords on five occasions, between 1748 and 1795. Each sword was named and numbered and all were identical in length, weight, and basic design. To catalogue the collection, he marked the blades with inscriptions of gold, silver, and copper to indicate the year, title, and series number of each piece. This sabre, named *Dexing* 德興 (Virtuous Dominance), was made in the fifty-eighth year of his reign (1793). It is number 27 in the earth series.

Portrait of Second-Rank Bodyguard Namjar
那木查爾像

Anonymous court painters
Hanging scroll, ink and colour on silk
Qing dynasty, 1760
Royal Ontario Museum, 923x56.8

The Imperial Banquet at the Pavilion of Purple Brightness
紫光閣賜宴圖卷

Yao Wenhan 姚文瀚 (active in the 18th century)
Handscroll, ink and colour on silk
Qing dynasty, 1761
The Palace Museum, Gu8242

Manchu emperors regularly held imperial military service exams and contests in archery, riding, and other skills at the Pavilion of Purple Brightness, northwest of the Forbidden City. In 1760, Emperor Qianlong ordered a renovation of the Pavilion to include a memorial hall commemorating his military victories over the Dzungars and Muslims. Inside the new hall, aside from displaying weapons and banners of the enemy, the emperor hung 100 scrolls showing life-sized portraits of honourable generals and soldiers who had sacrificed their lives in battle. *Portrait of Second-Rank Bodyguard Namjar* in the ROM collection came from this group.

Namjar is depicted in military attire, equipped with a quiver of arrows, a bow, and a broadsword. The distinctive features of his face—high cheekbones and damaged eyebrows—are striking. Yet his pose is more or less a stereotype found in the portrait series. Inscribed at the top in both Chinese (right) and Manchu scripts is a eulogy written in honour of the subject.

The long handscroll (see next page; detail at right) depicts vividly the celebration in 1761 at the completion of the renovated Pavilion (shown at the end of the long handscroll on pp.40-41). After a state banquet hosted by the emperor, the country's best skaters performed intricate acrobatic moves at high speed. Some skaters carry flags, while others carry a bow and arrows—racing to shoot backwards at a brightly coloured ball hanging from a wooden archway set up on the ice.

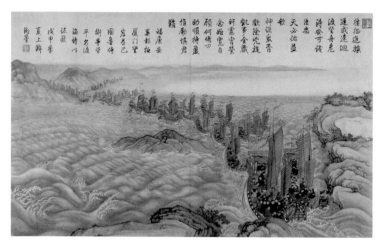

Battle Scenes from the Pacification of Taiwan
平定台灣戰圖冊

Qing court painters
Album, ink and colour on paper
Qing dynasty, Qianlong period
The Palace Museum, Gu6333-11/12

Emperor Qianlong liked to celebrate his military victories in images and texts. The album of the pacification of Taiwan, produced at the court, commemorates a successful seafaring military campaign undertaken in 1786–1788. The island of Taiwan (Formosa), located off the southeastern coast of China, did not appear on the map of the Qing imperial domain until 1683. In 1786, a rebellion led by Lin Wenshuang 林文爽 broke out. Emperor Qianlong had 6,000 soldiers sent by sea to pacify the rebellion because the local Qing government could not get it under control.

The twelve-sheet album vividly documents these battles from their outset to the capture of the rebel leader and the emperor's final reward banquet. In his commemorative poems inscribed on each leaf, the emperor also demonstrated his keen supervision throughout each battle, and the entire set showcases the great military achievements of the Qing under Qianlong's leadership.

Emperor Yongzheng Enjoying Himself
雍正帝行樂圖像冊

Anonymous court painter
Album, ink and colour on silk
Qing dynasty, 18th century
The Palace Museum, Gu6635-9/14

Although Emperor Yongzheng commissioned many
self-portraits in the genre of *xingle tu* 行樂圖 ("pictures of
enjoying pleasurable activities"), this fourteen-sheet album
presents the most idiosyncratic portraits of any Chinese
ruler in history. The emperor assumed various ethnicities
and characters, each accompanied by an animal or bird. Did
Yongzheng consider himself a universal monarch, embrac-
ing infinite space, time, and power? Was it just for the fun of
role-playing? Arguably the most fascinating emperor in the
Qing dynasty, Yongzheng's intention remains a mystery.

One leaf represents Yongzheng as a fisherman relaxing
with his eyes closed. He appears to be carefree, his fishing pole
suspended behind him, a basket already filled with fish at his
side. This persona might allude to the historical figure Jiang
Ziya 姜子牙 (better known as the Great Duke Jiang), the wise
man disguised as a fisherman who would only give advice to
those who were willing to "jump at the bait themselves."

Emperor Qianlong's copy of *Hungry Chicks* (Li Di, active in the 12th century)
仿李迪雞雛待飼圖卷

Hongli 弘曆 (Emperor Qianlong), 1711–1799
Handscroll, ink and colour on paper
Qing dynasty, 1788
The Palace Museum, Gu164612

In 1788, the fifty-third year of his reign, Emperor Qianlong copied a painting by the Southern Song court painter Li Di from 1197: two chicks attentively wait, mouths wide open, for food from their mother. The emperor did not copy Li Di's masterpiece for its artistic merit alone. In his eyes, the chicks represented thousands of starving victims of a devastating flood in the Jingjiang 荆江 area (modern Hubei 湖北 province) that year.

Qianlong skilfully turned an ordinary image into a symbolic statement of his benevolent rule, a key Confucian ideal of emperorship. To remind his local officials of this, he distributed rubbings of a carved stone version of both his painting and inscription nationwide. Embroidered copies, *kesi* (weft-woven silk painting) and *kemao* 緙毛 (weft-woven wool painting), were also made and displayed inside his palace, his summer retreat, and even his mausoleum.

The original poem inscribed by Qianlong to the left of Li Di's painting (as shown above) reads:

The two chicks seem to look around,
*   but where is their mother?*
Too young to peck grains all over the
threshing floor,

who will pity their starving stomachs?
Unfolding is a painting of paradigm;
*   all you see deserves deep reflection.*
The people in the disastrous land are
waiting to be fed;
*   the responsible officials must be vigilant!*

Prince Yinzhen Tilling and Weaving

胤禎耕織圖

Anonymous court painter
Album, ink and colour on silk
Qing dynasty
The Palace Museum, Gu6634-11, 42/52

The genre of Tilling and Weaving pictures had developed since the Southern Song dynasty (12th century) as a series of paintings with matching poems that were originally intended to document agricultural techniques and to provide step-by-step illustrations to both officials and commoners. Qing emperors valued and re-deployed the genre as a means to demonstrate the rulers' concerns for the people's livelihood and hardship.

Emperor Yongzheng commissioned this set of Tilling and Weaving pictures when he was still a prince. The set copied almost exactly an earlier series made by his father, Emperor Kangxi, who placed a great value on the work of commoners. The difference? Instead of showing farmers and weavers, Prince Yinzhen had himself and his consort depicted doing the work themselves. In doing this, he began to establish himself as a benevolent future ruler who knew first-hand the hardship of working to make a living.

Seal

"為君難" 壽山石螭鈕長方印

Stone
Qing dynasty, Yongzheng period
The Palace Museum, Gu166986

Emperor Yongzheng, the father of Qianlong, was the most hardworking emperor in the Qing court. His motto for himself was the phrase *weijun nan* 為君難 ("being the ruler is tough"), which was then carved on this seal. In 1723, the first year of Yongzheng's reign, the emperor requested that the Imperial Household Department make a hanging horizontal board with the calligraphy of these three characters and hang it at his new residence: the Hall of Mental Cultivation. The statement on the board was also reflected in his own antithetical couplet: "let the man (the Emperor) govern his people, not have his people serve the man" (惟以一人治天下, 豈為天下奉一人). At this emperor's wish, many copies of this seal were made to be placed in the different study rooms and to be given as gifts to his officials as a reminder of him being a diligent ruler.

Tally for the Imperial Gardens

銅圓明園八旗槍營合符

Gold-gilt brass
Qing dynasty, Tongzhi period
The Palace Museum, Gu166650

No one could pass through the gates of the Forbidden City at night unless they carried part of something called a tally. Each tally had two corresponding pieces, both carrying the words Imperial Edict (*shengzhi* 聖旨). On one piece, the words were raised. The senior guard at the gate held the other piece, on which the words were carved. Anyone who entered or left the Forbidden City had to have received the relief half of tally from the imperial officials. The visitor could pass only if the two pieces fit together.

The same security system was also applied to other imperial properties. The tally on display in this exhibition—only the relief half survives—was used in the summer palace, Yuanming yuan 圓明園. This particular tally was issued in the first year of Emperor Tongzhi (1862) and belonged to guards of the Firearm Battalion.

Two sides of one piece. The corresponding counter piece did not survive.

Rank badge, military
3rd degree, leopard
武官補子, 三品, 豹

Silk with gold and silver thread
Qing dynasty, 19th-20th centuries
Royal Ontario Museum,
950.100.15.B-C
Gift of Mrs. Sigmund Samuel

Rank badge, civilian
1st degree, crane
文官補子, 一品, 仙鶴

Silk tapestry
Qing dynasty, Kangxi period
Royal Ontario Museum,
950.100.124.B-C
Gift of Mrs. Sigmund Samuel

Throughout Ming and Qing dynasties, government officials wore square badges on the outside (front and back) of their dark surcoats to communicate their rank in the Chinese bureaucracy. Each of the nine grades in the civilian and military branches were represented by animals. The wives of these officials, as well as state censors and musicians, also communicated their status with badges.

Civilian officials—who attained rank only after a set of gruelling state exams—were represented by birds, perhaps because their wisdom brought them closer to the heavens. Military officials climbed the ranks through physical feats and were fittingly represented by strong mammals, including lions, bears, leopards, and mythical creatures.

All the intricacies of Chinese cosmology are expressed in rank badges, which were fashioned through tapestry and embroidery techniques, including extensive couching with gold thread. The general composition places the animal at the centre, while sky and clouds fill the upper reaches and waters rush below. The animal typically looks over its shoulder to a red sun disc, said to represent the emperor. Oftentimes, auspicious symbols—Taoist, Buddhist, Confucian—or wordplay are artfully inserted into the composition.

Over their 500 years of existence, the size, format, and aesthetics of these badges underwent dramatic transformations. Techniques, iconography, and border styles could change from decade to decade. For instance, auspicious symbols progressively crowded out other parts of the composition, until a reform code in the 1890s drastically simplified design (as shown on the badge with leopard).

LIFE IN THE PALACE

Imperial woman's riding jacket
貂皮琵琶襟馬褂

Silk, sable fur
Qing dynasty, Guangxu period
The Palace Museum, Gu49938

"Women hold the reins, spur on horses, and are no different from men ...
the wives and concubines are led into the hunt" (Manchu writing, pre-1644).

Embroidery, painting, and music were not the only skills developed by
Manchu women at court. Into the mid 1800s, both Manchu boys and girls
were trained in military horsemanship.

In the late 19th century men and women developed a fashion for
wearing riding jackets, *magua* 馬褂, over their robes as part of everyday
wear. These fashionable jackets might be constructed of costly fabrics,
such as silk, and elaborately decorated.

The pale green silk *magua* shown here, made for a court concubine,
follows the prevalent taste in the late Qing court for multiple contrasting
trims. The cuffs, collar, and hem of the brocaded silk fabric are edged with
rows of lace, black silk trim, and two shades of sable fur artfully combined
to create longevity symbols.

Detail from *Taking a Stag with a Mighty Arrow,* attributed to Giuseppe Castiglione, 1760s

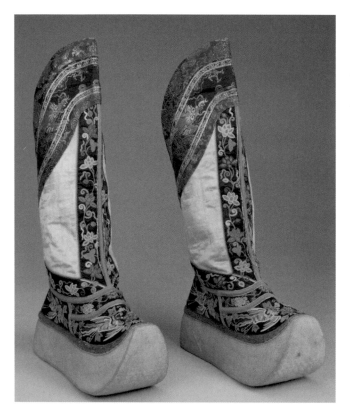

Empress's court boots
鳳凰紋皂靴

Silk, leather strips, wood, cotton
Qing dynasty, Kangxi period
The Palace Museum, Gu60211

Although normally hidden from view, a court woman's feet received as much thought and care as every other part of her body. Indeed, footware was a major means for expressing female ethnic identity, stature, and style.

Beginning in at least 1000 CE, elite Han women had their feet bound from a young age, preventing growth and creating tiny, stunted feet which they dressed in small silk slippers. Manchu women, on the other hand, were expressly forbidden from foot binding. Indeed, on ceremonial occasions, the empress wore sturdy equestrian boots similar to those of her imperial kinsmen. Yet even these boots could be made stylish, finely embroidered with floral shapes, birds, or mythical animals in silk, beads, or gold thread.

Manchu woman's shoes
雲紋頭尖底靴

Silk, wood, cotton, glass beads
Qing dynasty, Guangxu period
The Palace Museum, Gu61391

In their leisure moments, and as part of informal costume, Manchu women desired to emulate the short, mincing steps of the bound feet characteristic of women of the Han majority. As part of a growing tendency to blur differences in dress between the Han and Manchu, Manchu women came to fix their full-length slippers to platforms that measured up to 5 inches in height. Made of cotton stretched over wood, platform shapes varied and were given poetic names such as "ship's keel," "flowerpot," or "ingot." Platforms themselves became sites for aesthetic embellishment, decorated with glass beads or embroidery.

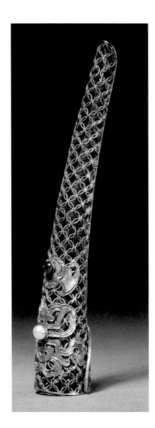

Woman's nail guards

銀鍍金珠石累絲指甲套

Gold-gilt silver, beads, gemstones
Qing dynasty
The Palace Museum, Gu225578-9

In Imperial China, top elites of the leisured class grew extremely long fingernails as an immediate sign that they did not need to labour manually. To protect these precious nails, and create an impression of elongated fingers, women toward the end of the Qing dynasty women developed a fashion for wearing nail guards.

Nail guards could be up to 6 inches long and were worn on the pinky and ring fingers of each hand. More than utilitarian coverings, they were fashioned from tortoiseshell, gold, silver, enamel, or gilt, often further embellished with filigree or inlaid jewels.

This pair from the Palace Museum is particularly resplendent. The guards are made of interlinking gilded silver wire, with inlaid pearls, red stones, and kingfisher feathers arranged to form the shapes of bats and *shou* characters.

Woman's informal coat with butterflies, attributed to Empress Dowager Cixi

傳慈禧 - 壽字蝶紋襯衣

Silk satin with silk embroidery
Qing dynasty, Guangxu Period
Royal Ontario Museum, 919.6.128
The George Crofts Collection. Gift of The Robert Simpson Co. Ltd.

As the top-ranking woman at court, the empress dowager Cixi was the Forbidden City's arbiter of fashion. She devoted special care and energy to choosing her unofficial dress, ordering every year some 160 bolts of silk, satin, gauze, and silk gauze from imperial workshops. For a five-day trip, Cixi's attendants might pack over 50 robes to accompany her.

For informal wear, Cixi preferred silks in saturated pastel shades—rather than imperial yellow, which she found unflattering for her skin tone—intricately embroidered with scattered bird or floral imagery. For her 1903 portrait by the American painter Katherine Carl, she wore a typical composition of grape clusters.

In 1919 the ROM acquired 35 informal women's robes attributed at the time to Cixi. Recent research suggests that two robes likely belonged to her, including this exquisitely embroidered "100 butterfly" robe lavishly worked with gold thread and *shou* characters.

The Empress Dowager Cixi
Katherine Carl
Oil on canvas
1903

Imperial dog outfit
紅色牡丹紋閃緞夾狗衣

Silk
Qing dynasty, Guangxu period
The Palace Museum, Gu62750

Many of the world's most popular lapdogs, such as the Pekinese *jinghabagou* 京哈吧狗 and pug, originated in China. In the Forbidden City, royal dogs received royal treatment. They reportedly lived in pavilions with marble floors, sleeping on silk cushions, tended by specialized eunuchs who worked for the Dog Raising Office. Court ladies in particular entertained themselves by walking, playing with, and dressing up their dogs. Empress Dowager Cixi was known to own dozens, making gifts of puppies adorned with silk leashes and harnesses. Every year, dozens of luxurious dog outfits were commissioned, the pet's name carefully recorded on the lining.

We thus know that this outfit was made during the Guangxu reign (1875–1908) for a hound named Dali 大利 (Big Luck). The brocaded silk fabric in a red, white, and purple peony pattern was tailored to cover the dog in its entirety, including its tail and snout.

Chopsticks, spoon, and fork

青玉鑲赤金筷, 青玉柄金匙, 青玉柄赤金叉

Jade and gold
Qing dynasty, Qianlong period
The Palace Museum, Gu11608, Gu11603, Gu11605

On special occasions, these exquisite eating utensils were used in the Palace of Eternal Longevity (Yongshou gong 永壽宮) by Emperor Qianlong's family and their guests. The palace, originally built in 1420 as part of the original Six-Western Palace in the Inner Court, was mostly occupied by the consorts of the emperors.

Inscribed on the handle of the spoon is the character meaning "double happiness," a typical blessing for a wedding. In the fifty-fourth year of Qianlong (1789), the emperor held a wedding banquet at this palace for his daughter, Princess Hexiao Gulun 固倫和孝公主, who married to a son of the Emperor's favourite officer, He Shen.

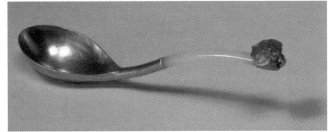

Hand warmer
黑漆描金山水樓閣圖手爐

Gold and black lacquer on wood
Qing dynasty, Yongzheng period
The Palace Museum, Gu113194

This hand warmer was clearly meant for the imperial use. The outer box was lavishly decorated with two large panels of landscapes inlaid with gold. Around them, gold-gilt paint created intertwining flowers. The elegant finish of the black lacquer wasn't very practical (the coating does not hold up well to heat). This was probably just a decorative piece, since there is no evidence of charcoal in the inner box.

Beginning in the late Ming dynasty, scholars used boxes like this to keep their hands warm while studying during cold winters. It was actually two boxes. Heated charcoal was placed in the metal interior, warming the space between it and the decorated outer box. The scholars wrapped their hands around the box, or held them above the lid, to feel the warmth.

Detail from a court painting showing a lady holding a hand warmer

Cricket jug

同治紫紅地粉彩題詩蟋蟀罐

Porcelain
Qing dynasty, Tongzhi period
The Palace Museum, Gu162370 4/25

Unlike bloody sports such as bullfighting and cockfighting, cricket fighting rarely causes injuries to the insects. It is a popular pastime or betting game in China which may date back more than 1,000 years, to the Tang dynasty.

Cricket fighting was a fascinating game for little royals; Emperor Tongzhi, who came to power at age 6, loved the game. This jug was specially made in the imperial kiln for the young emperor. It served two purposes. The nine small stackable containers within were used as cricket living compartments. When they were removed, the jug served as the arena for cricket fights.

Prince Yinzhen's painting of *Twelve Beauties*
十二美人圖軸

Anonymous court painter
Hanging scroll, ink and colour on silk
Qing dynasty, 18th century
The Palace Museum, Gu6548-10/12

Vase
白釉塑貼鮮紅蟠螭蒜頭瓶

Porcelain
Ming dynasty, Jiajing mark and period
The Palace Museum, Gu145720-10/12

Prince Yinzhen (future Emperor Yongzheng) had a series of gorgeous life-sized women painted for himself. These were originally mounted on a twelve-panel screen to surround a couch in the prince's favourite private study, the Deep Willows Reading Hall (Shenliu dushu tang 深柳讀書堂) at the Garden of Perfect Brightness (Yuanming yuan 圓明園).

Whether or not they represent Yinzhen's own concubines, the paintings of these "beauties" offer a glimpse into a concubine's private courtyard or boudoir, both places of romantic rendezvous. Many of the images are sexually appealing and contain symbols of love, such as butterflies or the small double-gourd held in the lady's hand in this picture. The lady looks directly at the viewer, inviting us to gaze at her charming willowy body leaning against a desk.

Items placed on the desk include a chessboard and an antique vase decorated with a raised *panchi* 蟠螭 motif (a type of dragon coiled around the body), which is similar to the one that once belonged to the imperial family and is still housed in the Palace Museum (right). Indeed, the vase is the rarest and finest example of Ming-dynasty porcelain from the 16th century. This unique type of vase with a garlic-shaped rim was used as a wine vessel and was no longer made (or if it was, no examples survive) when ceramic production peaked in the Qing dynasty. The high-quality furnishings (chessboard, antiques) are visual clues to the refinement of elite women and speak to the imperial taste.

STUDY AND COLLECTING

Ruyi charm
青玉刻乾隆御筆蘭亭帖如意
Jade
Qing dynasty, Qianlong period
The Palace Museum, Gu99701

Lacquer box
乾隆款剔紅曲水流觴圖扁圓盒
Lacquered wood
Qing dynasty, Qianlong period
The Palace Museum, Gu109821

The scene carved and illustrated on the head of this jade *ruyi* and on the lid of the red lacquer box is no ordinary gathering of intellectual minds. This was a historical gathering of some 42 scholars at the Spring Purification Festival during the Jin 晉 dynasty (265–420). Sitting around a flowing brook, they waited for cups of wine to float downstream. With each drink, they worked on composing a poem. Wang Xizhi 王羲之 (303–361), the most famous calligrapher in Chinese history, recorded the event in a preface to the participants' poems, thus beginning a long tradition of depicting the Orchid Pavilion gathering (*lanting xiuqi* 蘭亭修禊).

Centuries later, Emperor Qianlong participated in the timeless tradition by immortalizing the scene in many of his own writings and in the artworks he commissioned, including this *ruyi* and box. Incised on the handle of the *ruyi* is Wang's preface as written by Qianlong (originally filled with gold pigments). According to documents of the imperial household, the graphic on the lid of the lacquer box was kept as a model that would have been repeatedly used for designing other decorative objects.

Illustration by Emilio Genovese depicting the graphic on the head of the ruyi charm.

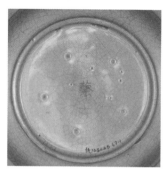

Ru ware dish
汝窯天青釉盤
Porcelain
Song dynasty, 960-1279 AD
The Palace Museum, Gu145445

Porcelain wares that were produced in the Song dynasty's state kiln, Ruzhou 汝州, in today's Henan 河南 province, are praised for both their artistic and technical achievement. *Ru* ware was one of five highly valued Song state porcelain wares. *Ru* ware became collectable in the Forbidden City court, and it was the only kind that Qing imperial kilns were not able to replicate. Today, fewer than 70 original pieces survived in the world, mostly in the collections of the Palace Museum in Beijing and the National Palace Museum in Taipei.

An incised mark, the surname Cai 蔡, is found on the bottom of this dish. Research suggests that the only family privileged enough to own such a dish must have been the family of Cai Jing 蔡京 (1047–1126), the powerful Primary Minister who served the last emperor of the Northern Song dynasty, Emperor Huizong.

Chicken cup
成化款鬥彩雞缸杯

Porcelain
Ming dynasty, Chenghua mark and period
The Palace Museum, Gu145644

A vivid scene of a rooster, hen, and two chicks in a garden is depicted on each side of this small wine cup. Such a "chicken cup" was made in the imperial kilns at Jingdezhen exclusively for the court of Emperor Chenghua. The empress dowager was particularly fond of small utensils and Chenghua took his mother's wishes very seriously. Thus, there were many small, light porcelains like this one produced during Chenghua's reign; more so than during any other. The beauty of the cup lies in the way colours were applied—both under and over the glaze, a technique called *doucai* 鬥彩. This required firing the cup twice at different temperatures.

Today only two original Chenghua chicken cups survive in the Palace Museum; there are fewer than a dozen in museum collections worldwide.

Embroidered painting
廣繡三羊開泰圖插屏心

Anonymous
Silk embroidery
Qing dynasty, Qianlong period
The Palace Museum, Xin67231

Numerous regional embroidery traditions are found in China. Of these, the Gu 顧 or Guangdong 廣東 style of the southern Canton port area became a favourite of the Qing court, which demanded pieces as tribute. These delicately embroidered scrolls, fans, and hangings were produced by men in workshops and intended as *objets d'art*. Likely influenced by Western painting, they are highly distinctive in both technique and imagery. Embroiderers used a vast range of colours and stitches to create delicate shading. Typically the composition is crowded with plants and animals that are associated with prosperity and are rendered in naturalistic forms. This piece depicts the well-known theme of three sheep, *san yang* 三羊, a homonym for the greeting of *sanyang kaitai* 三陽開泰 that expresses good wishes at the start of the new spring.

Cabbage-shaped vase
青玉白菜式花插

Jade
Qing dynasty
The Palace Museum, Gu98552

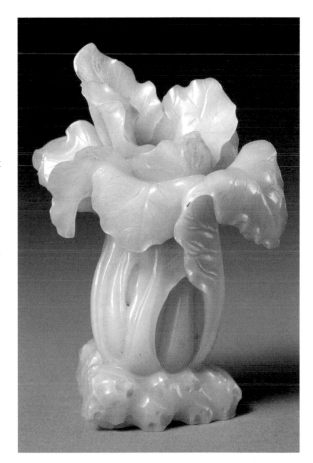

Jade vases or sculptures in the form of cabbage appeared often in the imperial collection because of the cabbage's sentimental value for Manchu people. Cabbage is the most common vegetation in northeast China, the home of the Manchu. Manchu people dried and salted cabbages in the fall, and relied on them for food over the long winter. An important mandate for each Manchu emperor was to always remind his people of their homeland and traditions, because their descendants were already assimilating to and heavily influenced by Han cultures and tradition.

Jades have been valuable and sentimental possessions to the Chinese for more than 8,000 years. Both Emperors Yongzheng and Qianlong were particularly fond of jade artworks. In order to control the imperial supplies, the Qing court regulated the mining, quarrying, and transportation of nephrite jade, the best quality of jade stone from the mountains in Hetian, China's far western land.

Jar
綠地粉彩藤蘿花鳥紋缸

Porcelain
Qing dynasty, Guangxu mark
and period
The Palace Museum, Gu157011

Design print
荷花鷺鷥魚缸圖樣

Anonymous court painter
Paper
Qing dynasty, 19th–early 20th century
The Palace Museum, Shu3425

Empress Dowager Cixi had a special collection of porcelains that only she could use in her personal studio, the Hall of Great Elegance (Dayazhai 大雅齋). Each piece was inscribed with a title and two specific phrases (*tiandi yijiachun* 天地一家春 and *yongqing changchun* 永慶長春), identifying it as a *Dayazhai* ware. The imperial kilns at Jingdezhen produced these special wares for Her Majesty between 1874 and 1907, ending their production just a year before she died.

The empress dowager had very particular tastes. To produce her personal *Dayazhai* porcelains, court artists painted their designs on sheets and sent them to her for approval. The prints defined the themes (here, it is flowers and birds), colours, and placement of inscriptions. Once Cixi approved the design, the Imperial Household Department sent a production order to the imperial kiln. The order specified the size, form, and quantity of each piece on a yellow strip beside the image.

Only 20 of these design prints survive. This particular design was ordered for production at least three times (there are three yellow order strips). One order (on the right) specified: "Using this design with pink ground-colours, make 20 extra-large bowls, 30 large bowls, 40 middle-sized bowls, and 60 small bowls. Also twenty 9-inch plates, thirty 7-inch plates, forty 5-inch plates, forty 3-inch plates."

FASCINATION WITH THE WEST

Auspicious Picture for the Dragon Boat Festival
午瑞圖

Giuseppe Castiglione (Chinese name Lang Shining 郎世寧) (1688-1766)
Hanging scroll, ink and colour on silk
Qing dynasty, 17th–18th centuries
The Palace Museum, Xin137132

Vase
天藍釉凸耳梅瓶

Porcelain
Qing dynasty, Kangxi mark and period
The Palace Museum, Gu147681

It was popular in the 17th and 18th centuries for well-to-do Chinese families to display "auspicious pictures" during seasonal festivals as a sign of blessings and good luck. What appears to be a "still life" here is such a seasonal picture. Glutinous rice wrapped in bamboo leaves (*zongzi* 粽子) was placed next to a vase with slender mugwort leaves (*aicao* 艾草) inserted among the flowers. These were the traditional food and plant of the Dragon Boat Festival (*duanwu* 端午), celebrated annually around the summer solstice.

Giuseppe Castiglione, arguably the most famous missionary artist in China, painted this painting in his early years serving in the Qing court. Here he used techniques typical of a European still life—steady composition, heavy colours, naturalistic flowers, a substantial vase—to portray a traditional Chinese subject. He captured the sheen of the glaze and smoothness of a sky-blue, narrow-necked vase (*meiping* 梅瓶), which was made in the Kangxi period and is displayed next to the painting in this exhibition.

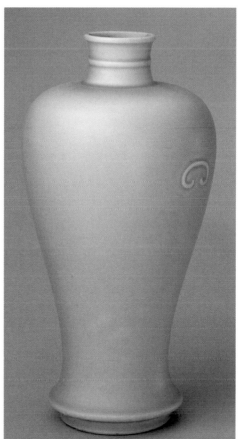

Musical clock
銅鍍金樂箱上亭式人打樂鐘

Made in Britain
Gold-gilt copper
Qing dynasty, 18th century
The Palace Museum, Gu182770

Mechanical clocks were introduced to Emperor Wanli by the Italian Jesuit Matteo Ricci 利瑪竇, who brought clocks into the Forbidden City in the 15th century as a gift to the court. As a result, British- and French-made clocks became the new fashion in the palace. Emperors Yongzheng and Qianlong ordered the Imperial Workshop (*Zhaoban chu* 造辦處) to produce Western-style clocks with traditional Chinese elements. Clock factories were established in Guangzhou, in southern China, with European technicians as supervisors. The clocks were meant for trade, but even the palace purchased them.

Clocks were the only foreign merchandise that Empress Dowager Cixi was so fond of. Emperor Guangxu was known for passing the time by rebuilding the inner workings of her many clocks in the palace when he was detained by Cixi after the failure of his reforms.

Incense burner

掐絲琺瑯纏枝蓮紋雙耳爐

Cloisonné enamel
Yuan dynasty, 1279–1368
The Palace Museum, Xin107409

This is one of the earliest examples of fine Chinese cloisonné, dated to the Yuan dynasty. The technique with enamels was imported to China from the west during the Yuan dynasty and quickly become fashionable and locally made during the Ming dynasty. The cloisonné was formed with enamel colouring material, glass, and metal wires on a metal body. Its manufacture was very time consuming, involving repeated application of enamels with low-temperature firing in a muffle kiln.

Incense burners in cloisonné forms became standard imperial utensils for most of the throne sets in the Forbidden City.

Plate

銅胎畫琺瑯花卉菱花形盤

Painted enamel on gold-gilt copper
Qing dynasty, Kangxi period
The Palace Museum, Gu116843 5/8

Incense Burner

畫琺瑯開光勾蓮紋三足爐

Painted enamel on metal
Qing dynasty, Yongzheng period
The Palace Museum, Gu116770

The plate (left) is from a set of eight enamel
plates in the collection of Emperor Kangxi.
According to the inscription on the
bottom, the colourful, rich-yellow enamelled ware was made at the imperial
workshop, under the direction of the
Emperor. Kangxi was the first emperor
who embraced and diligently studied
Western sciences and technology. In 1696,
the Emperor established the first glass
workshop in the palace, and later expanded
production to many areas including
enamelled products. He invited Western

technicians, introduced to him by French Jesuits, to supervise production and teach Chinese workers. During the Yongzheng period, the imperial workshop invented high-quality enamels from local materials. With this innovation, Chinese painted enamel ware reached its peak. The incense burner (right) dates to that peak period.

TWILIGHT OF THE LAST DYNASTY

Imperial seal
青玉交龍鈕 "皇帝之寶"

Jade
Qing dynasty, 17th–18th century
The Palace Museum, Gu166741

Emperor Qianlong was dissatisfied with 39 imperial seals he inherited because of their confusing titles and scope of use. In 1746, he selected 25 out of the 39 to be his imperial seals. He further selected 10 seals from the remaining 14, including this seal, the Treasure of the Emperor (*Huangdi zhibao* 皇帝之寶), to be placed at the Manchu's old palace at Shenjing 盛京 (modern-day Shenyang 瀋陽) in the North. The seal was later returned to the Forbidden City in 1900.

Symbols of legitimacy and power, the 25 primary imperial seals were inherited by each successive emperor after Qianlong and displayed in the Hall of Union (Jiaotai dian 交泰殿). On November 5, 1924, a day after the Last Emperor Puyi 溥儀 was forced to leave the palace, the set was handed over to the Government of the Republic, marking the end of the 2,000-year-old Chinese monarchy.

Inset: Interior of Hall of Union (jiaotai dian 交泰殿), where the 25 seals were placed and covered

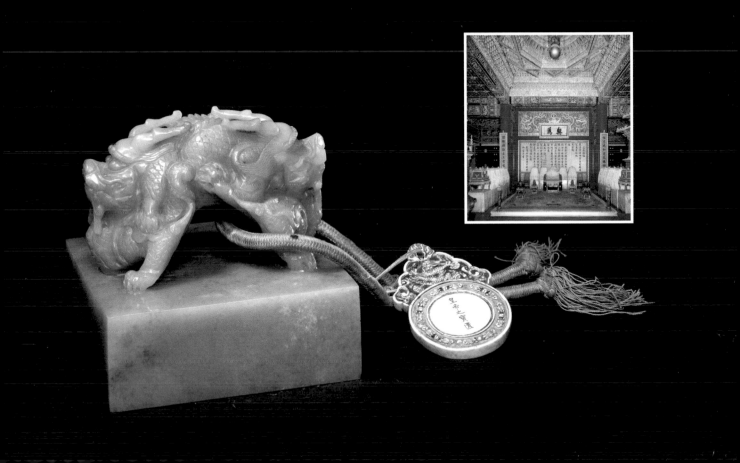

LECTURES & EVENTS

MARCH 27th ❧

CONTEXTS LECTURE

Gifts of Boundless Longevity: Imperial Birthday Celebrations within the Forbidden City

Dr Chen Shen

The Imperial Birthday Celebration was one of the three annual festivals at the Forbidden City during Qing dynasty, and was as important as both the lunar New Years Day and the Winter Solstice. At this time every year, tens of thousands of royal family members, officials, foreign envoys, and guests are gathered inside the Forbidden City for ceremonial celebrations that included banquets, music, opera performances, and fireworks. The most special event during the celebration was presentation of gifts between the Emperor and his guests. This talk will introduce festival events within the Forbidden City and some of the fine works of art in the ROM's exhibition that were once notable gifts for Imperial Birthdays.

SATURDAY, APRIL 26 ❧

Behind the Vermillion Walls: Courtly Life in the Inner Palace
(Bishop White Committee annual symposium)

The Bishop White Committee is sponsoring a one-day symposium focussing on the Forbidden City. The symposium will provide a rich exploration of the architecture, objects, and court life of the Forbidden City from ROM experts and distinguished colleagues.

MARCH–JUNE, 2014 ❧

Forbidden City Lecture Series

Explore Forbidden City series will present multiple perspectives and deeper exploration of themes from the exhibition, and will include experts from the ROM and around the world. Talks will compare and contrast the Forbidden City with other cities, palaces, and "taboo" places in the world, consider private life within the palace, and provide insight into the enduring legacy of imperial China in the East and West.

APRIL 12 AND 13 ❧

Chinese Heritage Weekend

SUNDAYS 1:30–3:30
FROM MARCH 25 THROUGH MAY 11 ❧

BRAINFOOD AT THE ROM

The World of the Dowager Empress: Late Dynasty China with George Hewson

By 1900, the widow of a late emperor has been the true ruler of China for over thirty years. Now foreign pressures are changing everything. What are her thoughts as she ponders the centuries of Chinese achievements and contemplates the country's uncertain future? Come see the ROM's outstanding Chinese gallery and hear the stories behind the objects on display.

MESSAGES FROM OUR SPONSORS

THE ROBERT H. N. HO FAMILY FOUNDATION PARTNERS WITH THE ROM TO PRESENT *FORBIDDEN CITY*

The Robert H. N. Ho Family Foundation is dedicated to promoting Chinese art and culture, and advancing cross-cultural understanding between China and the world. As the Presenting Sponsor of *The Forbidden City: Inside the Court of China's Emperors,* the Foundation is pleased to bring the stories of China's imperial palace to life at the ROM.

"For many decades it has been my personal goal to provide people in the West, particularly in Canada, with more and richer opportunities to appreciate Chinese culture. Eight years ago I established the Robert H. N. Ho Family Foundation to support cultural and educational projects such as this marvellous exhibition from Beijing's Palace Museum," said Robert H. N. Ho, founder of the Robert H. N. Ho Family Foundation.

The Forbidden City is complemented by robust educational programming that will encourage wider exploration by the public and young people, in particular school students. "Our Foundation emphasizes the educational aspect of exhibitions we support, hoping to advance cross-cultural insight and encourage popular appreciation for China's rich cultural heritage."

Many of the artworks featured in this stunning show have never been seen outside of China. In viewing these royal treasures, ROM visitors will learn about the history of China's last dynasties, including the governance of the Forbidden City, its relationship with the West, and its closing in 1911. *The Forbidden City* will make its Canadian premiere at the ROM and will commemorate the China-Canada Cultural Year.

何 鴻 毅 家 族 基 金
THE ROBERT H. N. HO FAMILY FOUNDATION

MANULIFE GENEROUSLY SUPPORTS *FORBIDDEN CITY* AS LEAD SPONSOR

Since welcoming its first customers more than 125 years ago, Manulife has grown into a leading global financial services group with principal operations in Asia, Canada, and the United States. Today, as part of its promise to build strong, vibrant communities, Manulife is proud to be the Lead Sponsor of *Forbidden City*.

"As a global company, Manulife is committed to engaging the international communities where we live and work," said Nicole Boivin, Senior Vice-President and Chief Branding and Communications Officer for Manulife. "We have been operating in China since 1897 and *The Forbidden City* exhibition is a true celebration of Chinese culture and its deep-rooted history."

A feast for the eyes, this beautiful show features approximately 250 rare objects from Beijing's celebrated Palace Museum. Many of these are national treasures never before seen in North America, augmented by objects from the ROM's own renowned collections.

"Partnering with the ROM to present this exclusive exhibition is a great way to honour the China-Canada Cultural Exchange in 2014, and commemorate the ROM's 100th anniversary."

Published by the Royal Ontario Museum with the generous support of the Louise Hawley Stone Charitable Trust. The Stone Trust generates significant annual funding for the Museum, providing a steady stream of support that is used to purchase new acquisitions and to produce publications related to the ROM's collections. The Louise Hawley Stone Charitable Trust was established in 1998 when the ROM received a charitable trust of nearly $50 million—the largest cash bequest ever received by the Museum—from its long-time friend and supporter, the late Louise Hawley Stone (1904–1997).

Royal Ontario Museum | 100 Queen's Park | Toronto, Ontario M5S 2C6
rom.on.ca

Library and Archives Canada Cataloguing in Publication

Cheng, Wen-chien, author
    The Forbidden City : inside the court of China's emperors / Wen-chien Cheng, Chen Shen.

Issued also in French under title: La Cité interdite.
Souvenir guide to accompany an exhibition held at the Royal Ontario Museum.
ISBN 978-0-88854-500-8 (pbk.)

    1. Forbidden City (Beijing, China)—Exhibitions. 2. Palaces—China—Beijing—Exhibitions. I. Shen, Chen, 1964-, author II. Royal Ontario Museum, host institution III. Title.

DS795.8.F67C44 2014   951'.156   C2014-900671-3

Chen Shen is Vice President, World Cultures, as well as Senior Curator and Bishop White Chair of East Asian Archaeology at the Royal Ontario Museum. Currently, his research focuses on human origins and ancient material cultures in East Asia Chen also teaches Art and Archaeology of Early China at the University of Toronto.

Wen-chien Cheng is the Royal Ontario Museum's Louise Hawley Stone Chair of Far Eastern Art. Her major area of research is pre-modern Chinese paintings, and her research approach is a contextualized study of visual culture. Wen-chien's most recent research examines issues of divergent female ideals in the paintings of women.

Sarah Fee is Curator of Eastern Hemisphere Textiles and Costume at the Royal Ontario Museum. With training in anthropology and African studies, Sarah's major research focuses on the island of Madagascar. Sarah, in her role as advisory curator for *The Forbidden City: Inside the Court of China's Emperors* exhibition, wrote about the textiles featured in the exhibition and in this guide.

Design: Ingrid Paulson
Art Director: Tara Winterhalt
Editor: Dimitra Chronopoulos
Managing Editor: Sheeza Sarfraz

Cover Photo: *Portrait of Emperor Yongzheng* (detail), colour on silk. Qing Dynasty, 1644-1911, © The Palace Museum, Gu6446.

Photos: © The Palace Museum: 10, 13, 15, 22, 24-29, 31-34, 36-37, 39-49, 53-56, 58-63, 65-71, 73-77, 79; Brian Boyle: 21, 23, 30, 33, 35, 38, 50-51, 57; Ingrid Paulson: 12.

Printed and bound in Canada.
The Royal Ontario Museum is an agency of the Government of Ontario.

FSC
www.fsc.org

MIX
Paper from
responsible sources
FSC® C011825